THE OFFICIAL
TOTTENHAM HOTSPUR™
ANNUAL 2007

A Grange Publication

© 2006. Published by Grange Communications Ltd., Edinburgh under licence from Tottenham Hotspur Football Club. Printed in the EU.

Written by Jonnie Baker

Photographs © Action Images

ISBN 0 9550057 5 2

£6.99

4

CONTENTS

MARTIN JOL

When Spurs beat Bolton 1-0 in the last game of the season at White Hart Lane, there was one man the fans wanted to hear from after the lap of honour.

Two words: Martin Jol.

The big Dutchman has brought a new optimism to the Lane and a confidence in the Lilywhites that has the fans singing his name and high-calibre players lining up to join the Jol revolution.

When he arrived in 2004, few Premiership followers had heard of Martin Jol but it didn't take long for him to make his mark, first as assistant to Jacques Santini and then as manager in his own right.

Leading Spurs into Europe via the league and turning them into genuine contenders for a Champions League spot – all while playing a brand of high tempo, passing football that excites the crowd and made the side a regular fixture on television.

An unsurpassed immersion in world football has also stood the former RKC Waalwijk manager in good stead. Anyone who heard his authoritative commentary during the World Cup couldn't fail to be impressed by his knowledge of individual players and teams.

The strong English spine of his Tottenham team is augmented by high quality foreign imports and is a testament to both his appreciation of world footballers and his determination to see Spurs upholding their traditional position as a giant of the English game.

On taking charge at Spurs, Jol reassured Spurs fans everywhere, that he knew where the heart of the great club lay.

Saying: "The players and I were at a memorial service for Bill Nicholson and we could not help but be inspired by the values and standards that he set and which we must try to regain."

As any Tottenham fan will tell you, the big Dutchman is well on his way to regaining those standards.

PORTSMOUTH 0	TOTTENHAM 2 (Griffin 45og, Defoe 64)
TOTTENHAM 2 (Defoe 49, Mido 75)	MIDDLESBROUGH 0
BLACKBURN 0	TOTTENHAM 0
TOTTENHAM 0 (Del Horno 39, Duff 71)	CHELSEA 2

AUGUST

After a busy summer in the transfer market, Tottenham's season was kick-started by an own goal at Pompey. A lacklustre opening half ended in bizarre fashion when Andy Griffin slid in on the on-rushing Mido and succeeded only in diverting the ball past Sander Westerveld in the Portsmouth goal. Though Pompey pressed hard for an equaliser the Spurs back four held out strongly and Jermain Defoe was on hand to sprint onto a through ball and round Westerveld for the second.

The flawless start to the Premiership continued when Middlesbrough arrived for the first game at White Hart Lane. Edgar Davids made his debut in a Spurs top and quickly stamped his authority on the midfield, while Defoe pulled out a stunning strike to impress the watching Sven Goran Eriksson. The speedy striker ran clear and let fly from 25 yards to leave Mark Schwarzer grasping at thin air. The keeper was to be beaten again when a tame shot from Mido wriggled under him and into the net.

By now Spurs fans were dreaming of Europe next season and a handy away point at a resurgent Blackburn Rovers bolstered the ambitions. Heavy pressure from the home side was confidently repelled by a determined Spurs defence and the Lilywhites returned to London with the point in the bag.

A win over Chelsea in the next game would have been the perfect end to the month, but the Blues ended up triumphant yet again. Despite matching the Premiership champions in the opening phases of the game, Spurs couldn't hold on after Mido was harshly dismissed for a challenge on Asier Del Horno. The Spanish wing back was on hand to grab the first before Damien Duff finished the job.

TOTTENHAM 0 LIVERPOOL 0	
ASTON VILLA 1 **TOTTENHAM 1**	
(Milner 4) **(Keane 78)**	
TOTTENHAM 1 FULHAM 1	
(Defoe 8)	

SEPTEMBER

The team's first chance to test themselves against possible rivals for a Champions League place came with the visit of Liverpool to the Lane. And the game was to end goalless despite disallowed goals from Defoe and Liverpool's Crouch. A magnificent performance from Carrick alongside deadline day signing Jermaine Jenas, was a shining light for the Lilywhites.

Spurs then traveled to Villa Park and picked up another priceless point on the road. After going behind to a goal from on-loan winger Milner, Tottenham could have been in trouble. But Robbie Keane scored a magnificent equaliser to ensure a share of the spoils.

Keane's strike partner Jermain Defoe was to prove the hero when Fulham came calling. A lovely ball from club captain Ledley King allowed Defoe to slip through the Cottagers defence and slot the ball past keeper Tony Warner.

OCTOBER

CHARLTON 2 (Bent 25,48)	TOTTENHAM 3 (King 51, Mido 64, Keane 80)
TOTTENHAM 2 (Mido 58, Jenas 63)	EVERTON 0
MANCHESTER UNITED 1 (Silvestre 7)	TOTTENHAM 1 (Jenas 72)
TOTTENHAM 1 (King17)	ARSENAL 1 (Pires 77)

When Spurs went 2-0 down in the London derby away to Charlton, it looked like Martin Jol's side were going to be sent back to the Lane empty handed. But the Valley side hadn't counted on Tottenham's powers of recovery.

Captain King stepped up to pull one back, Mido bagged the equaliser following the deftest of reverse passes from Tainio and Robbie Keane drove in the winner. Three points.

With Tottenham on a high following their magnificent comeback away to Charlton, Everton were right to be nervous about visiting White Hart Lane. The Toffees held onto until 13 minutes into the second half when Mido headed home from a Jenas cross. Jenas added the second five minutes later.

A visit to Old Trafford threatened to derail the bright start to the season, and when Silvestre netted in the seventh minute Spurs could have crumbled. But Martin Jol's side pulled it round and Jenas notched a glorious free kick to take another point away.

Old enemies Arsenal were the final visitors to the Lane in October and Spurs were disappointed to only take a point. A dominant performance in the first half saw Ledley King head powerfully home but the Gunners were fortunate to take a point when Robert Pires took advantage of a defensive slip up to equalise.

NOVEMBER

BOLTON 1 (Nolan 32)	**TOTTENHAM 0**
TOTTENHAM 1 **(Mido 16)**	**WEST HAM 1** (Ferdinand 90)
WIGAN 1 (McCulloch 88)	**TOTTENHAM 2** **(Keane 8, Davids 77)**

Come November and Spurs were finally to lose on the road, when the Reebok Stadium proved a bridge too far. But they could count themselves unlucky to leave the North West without a point after Jermain Defoe's finish was harshly judged offside.

A dominant performance at home to West Ham was also to end in disappointment. Mido was on hand to score his fourth of the season, a beautifully judged header from the edge of the area leaving the Hammers' keeper Shaka Hislop stranded. But young defender Anton Ferdinand nipped in in stoppage time to snatch an equaliser for the visitors.

After two disappointing games, many were tipping Tottenham to struggle when they traveled to the JJB Stadium to take on the season's surprise package Wigan. But a magnificent performance from Martin Jol's men saw them take all three points home with them. Robbie Keane finished well to establish an early lead and Edgar Davids lashed home his first for his new club to seal the win. A late consolation for Wigan wasn't enough to dent Spurs spirits.

DECEMBER

TOTTENHAM 3 (Mido 37, Keane 51 Carrick 77)	SUNDERLAND 2 (Whitehead 16, Le Tallec 60)
TOTTENHAM 3 (King 57, Mido 85 Defoe 90)	PORTSMOUTH 1 (Lua Lua 24)
MIDDLESBROUGH 3 (Yakubu 30,43 Queudrue 69)	**TOTTENHAM 3** (Keane 25, Jenas 63, Mido 83)
TOTTENHAM 2 (Keane 58, Defoe 90)	BIRMINGHAM 0
WEST BROM 2 (Kanu 23,52)	**TOTTENHAM 0**
TOTTENHAM 2 (Tainio 43, Mido 66)	NEWCASTLE 0

December is always a test of a team's league ambitions, and the festive period was to rubber stamp Tottenham's impressive form.

Michael Carrick's first goal for Spurs killed off a spirited challenge from Sunderland. The Black Cats had taken the lead only to be overhauled thanks to goals from Mido and Keane. Le Tallec's equaliser was the cue for a Tottenham onslaught that brought the glory to Carrick.

With Harry Redknapp reinstalled at Pompey, he would rather not have faced an on-song Spurs side in his first game in charge. LuaLua's speculative shot had given his side the lead but King, Mido and Defoe all struck to make it six points out of six.

A trip to the Riverside is always a challenge but few expected Tottenham's visit to serve up a Premiership classic. Spurs simply refused to be beaten and could have snatched all three points at the death.

The Boxing Day visit of Birmingham brought little Christmas cheer for Blues, once again Keane and Defoe took the plaudits despite a determined display from the visitors.

But there was to be disappointment at the Hawthorns, former Arsenal man Kanu scored twice to send Spurs to only their second away defeat of the season.

Newcastle may have thought Tottenham would be downbeat after defeat to West Brom, but it was business as usual at the Lane. Tainio grabbed his first goal in a Spurs strip and Mido volleyed over Shay Given to send the Magpies home empty-handed.

MANCHESTER CITY 0	**TOTTENHAM 2** (Mido 31, Keane 83)
LIVERPOOL 1 (Kewell 59)	**TOTTENHAM 0**
TOTTENHAM 0	ASTON VILLA 0
FULHAM 1 (Bocanegra 90)	**TOTTENHAM 0**

JANUARY

SEASON REVIEW

When January arrived Spurs were starting be talked of as genuine contenders for a Champions League place and an excellent showing against Man City only reinforced that view.

Mido slotted home after the always exciting Aaron Lennon had raced by Sylvain Distin to cut the ball back for the Egyptian striker. Then Keane finished it off, bringing down Mido's flick on with customary style and firing past David James.

After drawing with Liverpool at the Lane, Martin Jol's side had high hopes of taking at least a point from their visit to Anfield. But it wasn't to be, despite a resilient and, at times, dominant performance. It took an outstanding volley from Kewell to end the Tottenham resistance.

The visit of Aston Villa to North London was an excellent chance to bounce back from the defeat at Liverpool and Spurs threw everything at the Midlanders. But despite battering Villa, Spurs simply couldn't find a way past an inspired Thomas Sorensen in the Villa's goal.

After losing a last minute goal at home to West Ham, it was doubly galling when Carlos Bocanegra headed home to steal the points in the London derby. Spurs could have had a penalty earlier in the second half and were desperately unlucky to be left without a point.

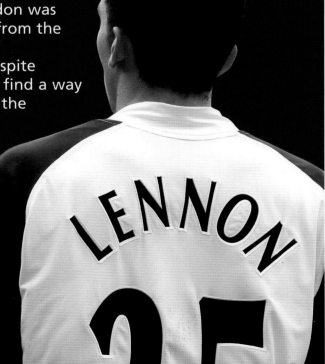

FEBRUARY

TOTTENHAM 3 **(Defoe 14, 46** **Jenas 41)**	CHARLTON 1 (Thomas 70)
SUNDERLAND 1 (Murphy 89)	**TOTTENHAM 1** **(Keane 38)**
TOTTENHAM 2 **(Mido 23, Defoe 68)**	WIGAN 2 (Johansson 10,67)

Jermain Defoe was the man of the moment when Charlton turned up at the Lane. Beautifully taken goals in each half from the England international striker and a calmly slotted goal from Jenas were enough to put paid to the Charlton challenge. A consolation from Jerome Thomas did little to dent the optimistic mood in North London.

Yet another last minute goal was to prove Tottenham's undoing at the Stadium of Light. Despite dominating the game, Spurs were unable to add to Robbie Keane's first half strike and when Darryl Murphy scored in the closing stages, it was two points dropped on the road.

The Lilywhite's determination was brought to the fore when Wigan put on an outstanding display to take a point from their trip to White Hart Lane. The newly promoted side twice took the lead but Spurs struck back on both occasions. Mido and Defoe took the plaudits while Wigan cemented their reputation as the surprise side of the season.

TOTTENHAM 3	BLACKBURN 2
(Keane 9, 42	(Sinama Pongolle 44,
Mido 70)	Bellamy 67)
CHELSEA 2	**TOTTENHAM 1**
(Essien 14,	**(Jenas 45)**
Gallas 90)	
BIRMINGHAM 0	**TOTTENHAM 2**
	(Lennon 65, Keane 77)
TOTTENHAM 2	WEST BROM 1
(Keane 68, 89)	(Davies 21)

MARCH

With the season drawing to a close, Spurs were still in the hunt for the Champions League and showing no intention of giving up fourth spot.

Blackburn pushed them hard, but two goals from Keane – one a contender for goal of the season – and a timely finish from Mido after a blistering run from Aaron Lennon were enough to send the Rovers away defeated.

A meeting with Chelsea was the next fixture for Tottenham and they came desperately close to taking a point from their bogey side. A last minute piledriver from Gallas sealed the points but the reigning champions were plainly troubled by Martin Jol's side.

It was Birmingham who felt the backlash from the Chelsea defeat, with Aaron Lennon netting his first goal for Spurs and Keane converting an inch perfect pass from Jenas. Despite being away from home, the North Londoners had stamped their authority all over a game in which they were rarely troubled.

And it was another Midland side that were to be the next victims, as West Brom fell to a late Keane penalty. Curtis Davies headed the Baggies ahead before Keane got on the end of magnificent pass from Carrick to slot the equaliser. Then when keeper Kuszczak brought down Defoe, Keane made no mistake from the penalty spot.

APRIL

NEWCASTLE 3 (Bowyer 2, Ameobi 25 Shearer 30)	**TOTTENHAM 1** **(Keane 19)**
TOTTENHAM 2 **(Stalteri 44, Carrick 49)**	MANCHESTER CITY 1 (Samaras 52)
EVERTON 0	**TOTTENHAM 1** **(Keane 33)**
TOTTENHAM 1 **(Jenas 53)**	MANCHESTER UNITED 2 (Rooney 8, 36)
ARSENAL 1 (Henry 84)	**TOTTENHAM 1** **(Keane 66)**
TOTTENHAM 1 **(Lennon 60)**	BOLTON 0

Six games in April would go along way to shaping Tottenham's Champions League destiny and the month got off to a bizarre start on April Fools Day. The scoreline may have ended 3-1 in favour of Newcastle, but Spurs easily deserved a point. A harsh red card for Michael Dawson was a further blow.

But in a season where Spurs were never to lose two league games in a row, the side once again bounced back. This time it was Manchester City who were on the receiving end when Paul Stalteri scored his first league goal for the club and Michael Carrick stepped forward from midfield to clinch the points.

A 1-0 win at Everton gave Martin Jol and his players more heart and the performance was even more encouraging than the scoreline. A Robbie Keane penalty separated the sides but Spurs could easily have won by three or more such was their control.

With Manchester United desperately trying to chase down Chelsea at the top of the league, the Red Devils visit to the Lane was going to be difficult for Spurs. Despite being the better team for long periods of the game, the home side were left disappointed.

Then the big one, with Arsenal still four points behind Spurs, the Gunners were desperate for a result against their London rivals. But they weren't to get it in the last ever North London Derby at Highbury. Tottenham dominated their neighbours and were disappointed to be pegged back and only take a point.

In the last game of the season at White Hart Lane, Spurs were still chasing the Champions League and were glad to run out 1-0 winners thanks to Aaron Lennon's beautifully taken goal.

A tumultuous welcome greeted the players in their lap of honour.

May 7 was a day of destiny for Tottenham, match Arsenal's result at home to Wigan and they would finish fourth and qualify for the Champions League.

But it wasn't to be, with the Gunners winning 4-2 in their last game at Highbury, Spurs needed a win, however circumstances conspired against them.

An outbreak of illness in the squad left the team weakened and heroic performances from Michael Dawson and the rest of the side wasn't enough to haul them over the line.

Goals from Fletcher and Benayoun knocked the stuffing out of the depleted team and despite a smart finish from Defoe, Tottenham couldn't finish the job.

It was a heartbreaking end to a quite magnificent season for the boys from White Hart Lane.

WEST HAM 2	TOTTENHAM 1
(Fletcher 10 Benayoun 80)	(Defoe 35)

SEASON QUIZ

1 Name the two players who scored for Tottenham against arch-rivals Arsenal

2 Who scored for Spurs in the ill-fated FA cup tie with Leicester? And who bagged the winner for the Foxes?

3 Which Serie A team was Egyptian striker Mido on loan from?

4 Which ex-Liverpool player joined the club in the last minutes of the January transfer window?

5 And which club did he join from?

6 Who scored the goal against Bolton that kept the Champions League dream alive?

7 Against which team did Edgar Davids score his first goal for Tottenham?

Answers on page 61

LEDLEY KING

Every side needs a rock to build themselves around and for Tottenham it's the man at the back that gives them strength.

Ledley King is Spurs through and through and has accepted the mantle of club captain with the quiet grace and determination for which he's become well known.

Blessed with natural pace and an impressive calmness on the ball, Ledley has won international recognition with England both in the centre of defence and as a holding midfielder where his ability on the ball allows him to break up attacks and start the counters.

Born in Bow in 1980, Ledley officially joined Tottenham in 1997 as a trainee and signed on as a professional the following year, making his debut away to Liverpool in 1999.

He replaced Jamie Redknapp as captain in 2005 and has made 204 appearances for Spurs in all competitions.

The 6 feet 2 inch defender is also a powerful attacking force and scored with a header in last season's North London derby - he has also scored one of the quickest ever Premiership goals, netting inside 10 seconds of kick off in the 3-3 game with Bradford in December 2000.

Having formed a steadfast partnership with new boy Michael Dawson at the heart of the Spurs defence, Tottenham were eager to hold onto their captain amid rumours of a move away.

Chelsea and Liverpool were both said to be keen to buy Ledley, but Martin Jol and Spurs were not prepared to lose one of the jewels in the White Hart Lane crown.

So it was with great delight that Spurs fans greeted the news in May that their captain had signed on to stay at White Hart Lane.

After signing the contract extension King explained why he was so happy to have secured his future with Spurs.

"I am thoroughly enjoying my football at Tottenham," he said, "It has been a terrific season, one of the best ever whilst I have been at the club. We are a club with a very bright future and I am looking forward to playing a part in that."

And Ledley wasn't the only one happy to see his name on a new contract, manager Martin Jol made no secret about how important his captain is to the club.

"Ledley is without doubt one of the most impressive and talented players not just in this country, but in Europe," said the Dutchman.

"We know that so many other clubs would love to lure him from us so we are really pleased he has agreed a new deal. We often tease him that he has blue and white blood – he came to this club as a youngster 11 years ago and we have been privileged to have seen him develop with us and represent the club for seven years

"Loyalty is a rare commodity. Ledley is an outstanding role model for our youngsters. We have never taken his commitment to this club for granted and we always seek to reward our best players with improved contracts," he added.

High praise, but praise that Ledley has earned with performance after performance for the club he loves.

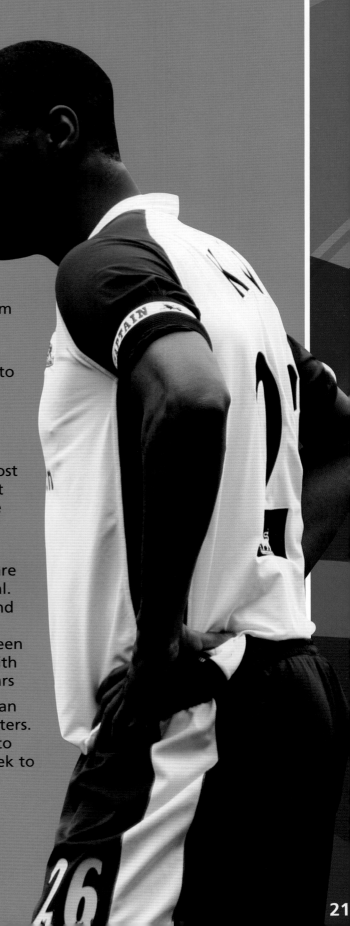

SPOT THE DIFFERENCE

1

Find 6 differences
between these photos.

2

Answers on page 61

WORDSEARCH

Find the words in the grid. Words can go horizontally, vertically and diagonally in all eight directions.

K	J	W	A	D	D	L	E	N	O	S	W	A	D	N
L	H	C	C	O	C	K	E	R	E	L	P	E	S	O
G	O	F	K	K	T	X	T	L	E	J	N	H	E	T
G	D	H	E	K	W	F	L	D	E	A	Y	V	V	X
H	D	G	M	N	L	K	L	K	L	V	O	M	E	A
L	L	M	A	E	A	E	G	T	T	T	Y	S	N	P
G	E	N	H	S	Y	E	R	I	A	L	T	T	S	W
R	J	S	N	N	C	A	K	B	N	A	N	H	I	P
P	B	R	E	L	H	O	R	R	L	O	R	N	S	L
L	Q	C	T	E	C	E	I	T	U	M	L	L	T	O
T	D	F	T	D	B	T	E	G	K	P	G	A	E	J
X	T	I	O	L	L	R	H	H	N	N	S	D	R	J
B	H	R	T	D	I	W	N	Q	Z	E	K	T	S	R
W	V	J	Q	M	R	O	B	I	N	S	O	N	O	Z
R	E	W	O	L	F	H	C	N	A	L	B	D	K	H

BERBATOV
BLANCHFLOWER
COCKEREL
DAWSON
GASCOIGNE
GINOLA
HODDLE

HOTSPUR
JOL
KEANE
LEDLEY
LEVY
PAXTON
ROBINSON

SEVENSISTERS
SHELF
STALTERI
TOTTENHAM
WADDLE
WHITEHARTLANE

Answers on page 61

CROSSWORD

ACROSS

2   Shirt Manufacturer (4)
3   Spurs win when there's a
    one in the year (2,3)
5   Ex-striker, Gary (7)
7   Martin ___ (3)
8   Former player, now sports
    presenter, Garth (6)
9   Last season's leading scorer (6,5)
11 New shirt sponsor (7)
12 Jet-heeled winger and England
    international, Aaron (6)

DOWN

1   Home of Spurs, Hart Lane (5)
2   England's number one (4,8)
4   Ex-captain, Steve (8)
5   Tottenham club captain (6,4)
6   Signed from Bayer Leverkusen
    in £10 million deal, Dimitar (8)
10 Spurs mascot (6)
12 Chairman, Daniel (4)

Answers on page 61

RESERVE LEAGUE CHAMPIONS

Every successful Premiership side needs to have strength in depth and Spurs can boast just that after the Reserve Team staged a triumphant march to the Barclays Premier Reserve League South title.

Lead by striking legend Clive Allen, the reserves carried all before them in their charge to the title and had the comfort of clinching the trophy with games to spare.

2005

BAR

A run of 14 wins in 15 games was the form that clinched the title for Allen's boys and they had the pleasure of beating Arsenal to the trophy.

When results meant that Clive's side were in an unassailable position at the top of the table he was unable to disguise his delight.

On the night that Spurs were guaranteed the championship he said: "I'm delighted for everyone and it's been a fantastic team effort."

He added: "We've made great strides this season. I said to the lads on day one that I wanted to win this title, they wanted the same and they've done it in style.

"I'm proud and privileged to have led this group to the championship."

2006

TOTTENHAM HOTSPUR

LAYS

STADIUM PROFILE

WHITE HART LANE

INAUGURATED: 1899

CAPACITY: 36,200

RECORD ATTENDANCE: 75,038; vs Sunderland, March 5 1938

ADDRESS: Bill Nicholson Way, 748 High Road,
Tottenham, London, N17 0AP

Spurs moved to White Hart Lane in 1899 and have been playing there ever since. The famous pitch is overlooked by a copper fighting cock, the club's symbol, which is still in pride of place on the roof of both the West and East Stand.

Often known as The Lane, the stadium is one of the most evocative grounds in English football and has long been known as a home of stylish, passing football.

TOP GOALS

ROBBIE KEANE: TOTTENHAM 3 BLACKBURN ROVERS 2

If it's a spectacular goal you're looking for, Robbie Keane's a good man to turn to and he certainly turned it on in the home game with Blackburn. With three points a necessity as Spurs pushed on towards possible Champions League qualification, an early goal would be a bonus against a Blackburn side who were making their own charge for Europe. And Keane was the man to provide it in the ninth minute.

Taking a throw in from Mido close to the byline, the Republic of Ireland star flipped the ball over Robbie Savage and left Lucas Neill for dead. With Brad Friedel rushing out to meet him, Keane calmly slotted the ball past the American keeper to open the scoring and pave the way to a vital win.

JERMAINE JENAS: MANCHESTER UNITED 1 TOTTENHAM 1

In seasons past, a trip to Old Trafford would have been a daunting prospect for Spurs, but the boys from White Hart Lane are made of sterner stuff these days and they picked up a valuable point thanks to an exquisite Jenas free kick. Tottenham were trailing to a unfortunate goal, when Rio Ferdinand brought down Jenas more than twenty yards from the Manchester United goal. Stepping up to take the free kick, Jenas struck the ball sweetly and curled it past the despairing Edwin Van der Sar and into the top corner. One apiece and Tottenham were back on track for another valuable away point.

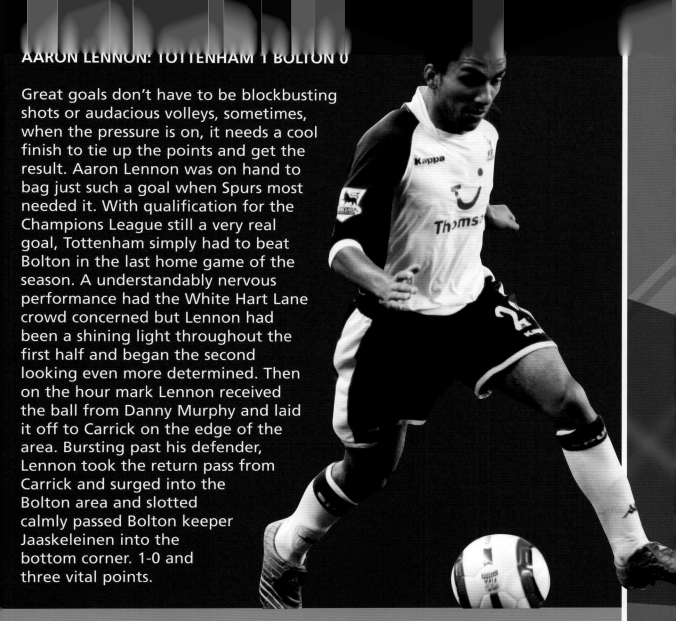

AARON LENNON: TOTTENHAM 1 BOLTON 0

Great goals don't have to be blockbusting shots or audacious volleys, sometimes, when the pressure is on, it needs a cool finish to tie up the points and get the result. Aaron Lennon was on hand to bag just such a goal when Spurs most needed it. With qualification for the Champions League still a very real goal, Tottenham simply had to beat Bolton in the last home game of the season. A understandably nervous performance had the White Hart Lane crowd concerned but Lennon had been a shining light throughout the first half and began the second looking even more determined. Then on the hour mark Lennon received the ball from Danny Murphy and laid it off to Carrick on the edge of the area. Bursting past his defender, Lennon took the return pass from Carrick and surged into the Bolton area and slotted calmly passed Bolton keeper Jaaskeleinen into the bottom corner. 1-0 and three vital points.

EDGAR DAVIDS:
WIGAN 1 TOTTENHAM 2

All eyes were on Holland legend Edgar Davids when he joined Tottenham, but he wasn't to open his scoring account until the visit to Wigan Athletic. Wigan had proved to be the surprise package of the Premiership season and it was a real test for the newly resurgent Tottenham with few pundits expecting them to take full points from the JJB stadium. But Spurs were in control from the start and Robbie Keane gave his side the lead as early as the eighth minute. With Martin Jol's men so dominant it was important to push the advantage home and the forceful Davids did just that. Taking the ball just inside the Wigan half he drove forcefully towards the home goal. With Wigan backing off he continued into the area before lashing the ball home past the diving Mike Pollitt.

ANDY REID

DOB: 29/ 7/ 82
POSITION: MIDFIELDER
PREVIOUS CLUB: NOTTINGHAM FOREST

A naturally left-sided midfielder, Andy Reid joined Tottenham on the last day of the January transfer window in 2005 in a deal which also saw clubmate Michael Dawson sign on at White Hart Lane. Playing predominantly as a left winger, the Ireland international scored his first Tottenham goal in the 5-1 demolition of Aston Villa on May 1, 2005. Reid can also play on the right of midfield and behind the strikers.

ANTHONY GARDNER

DOB: 19/9/80
POSITION: DEFENDER
PREVIOUS CLUB: PORT VALE

Anthony Gardner was one of the most sought after young players in England when he joined Spurs from Port Vale in January 2000. Since then, the towering centre back has developed into an important and dependable member of the squad at White Hart Lane. A series of unfortunate injuries have sometimes derailed his development but he made 18 appearances in 2005/06 and was particularly impressive away to Arsenal during the chase for Champions League qualification. Surprisingly quick for such a tall player, Gardner proved more than a match for the speed of Thierry Henry.

DANNY MURPHY

DOB: 18/3/77
POSITION: MIDFIELD
PREVIOUS CLUBS: CREWE ALEXANDRA, LIVERPOOL, CHARLTON ATHLETIC

Danny Murphy joined Tottenham at the second time of asking, having originally joined Charlton when he left Liverpool at the start of the 2004/05 season. After performing well at the Valley, the versatile midfielder was tempted to White Hart Lane in January 2006 on transfer deadline day. Comfortable in central midfield, wide or playing behind a front two, Murphy is well known for his ability to find a defence splitting pass or slot accurate free kicks.

EDGAR DAVIDS

DOB: 13/3/73
POSITION: MIDFIELDER
PREVIOUS CLUBS: AJAX, AC MILAN,
JUVENTUS, BARCELONA,
INTER MILAN.

The arrival of Edgar Davids in August 2005 was a vital moment for the Spurs side being built by his fellow countryman Martin Jol. As well as his barnstorming performances on the park the Dutchman, nicknamed the Pitbull, has been credited by the club's younger players with contributing enormously to their development as professionals. A huge hit with the fans, Davids scored once in 31 appearances in 2005/06 – netting with a powerful shot during the side's 2-1 away victory over Wigan.

JERMAIN DEFOE

DOB: 7/10/82
POSITION: STRIKER
PREVIOUS CLUBS: WEST HAM UNITED,
BOURNEMOUTH (LOAN)

One of the most naturally talented finishers in the country, Defoe joined Spurs in February 2004 and quickly made his mark. Having joined West Ham in 1999 Defoe made his mark on the Premiership and signed for Tottenham for £7 million after the Hammers were relegated. Lightning quick and deadly in one-on-ones with opposing goalkeepers, Jermain is one of the most sought after frontmen in the country. He netted nine times in the 2005/06 season.

JERMAINE JENAS

DOB: 18/2/83
POSITION: MIDFIELDER
PREVIOUS CLUBS: NOTTINGHAM FOREST,
NEWCASTLE UNITED

JJ is one of the most highly rated midfielders in the country and boasts a box-box goalscoring touch. A regular member of the England international squad, Jermaine travelled to Germany for the World Cup after impressing during an England tour to the USA. A beautifully taken free kick away to Manchester United cemented his position as a fan favourite at White Hart Lane. Playing either on the right or through the centre of midfield he brings energy and drive to the Spurs first eleven.

CALUM DAVENPORT

DOB: 1/1/83
POSITION: DEFENDER
PREVIOUS CLUBS: COVENTRY,
WEST HAM (LOAN), SOUTHAMPTON (LOAN), NORWICH CITY
(LOAN).

One of the rising stars of the Martin Jol revolution at Tottenham, Calum Davenport typifies the club's policy of investing in the best of young, British talent. A commanding centre back, Calum joined at the start of the 2004/05 season before gaining valuable experience on loan. He made his league debut in last season's home game with Manchester United and while Spurs were unlucky to lose the match, Davenport showed the fans he's an able replacement in our backline. A key figure in last season's cup winning reserve side, the Bedford-born defender is now ready to push for a spot in the first team.

MICHAEL DAWSON

DOB: 18/11/83
POSITION: DEFENDER
PREVIOUS CLUB: NOTTINGHAM FOREST

Dawson joined Spurs in the deal that also brought Andy Reid to the Lane and quickly became a favourite with the fans. The young centre half is one of the most exciting talents in the country and plays with a whole-hearted determination that has endeared him to fans and pundits alike. Forming a watertight partnership with club captain Ledley King, Dawson is now surely one of the first names on Martin Jol's team sheet. Having recently signed a new deal with Tottenham he looks set to develop into an England regular and Spurs stalwart.

PAUL ROBINSON

D.O.B: 15/10/79
POSITION: GOALKEEPER
PREVIOUS CLUB: LEEDS UNITED

England's number one and a favourite with Spurs fans, Paul Robinson joined the club from Leeds in the summer of 2004. The Beverley-born keeper is the rock on which the Spurs defence has been built and is now first choice goalkeeper for the national side. After committing his long-term future to the club, Robinson is set to bring the European experience he gained with Leeds to Tottenham's UEFA cup campaign.

RADEK CERNY

DOB: 18/2/74
POSITION: GOALKEEPER
PREVIOUS CLUBS: CESKE, CHEB, SLAVIA PRAGUE

As number two goalkeeper at Tottenham, Radek Cerny is one of the unsung heroes of the side. A full international with the Czech Republic, Cerny has extended his loan spell from Slavia Prague until the end of the 2007/08 season and has impressed when deputising for Paul Robinson. The experienced custodian also played a part in the reserve team's title winning exploits, appearing for the second string on nine occasions.

TEEMU TAINIO

DOB: 27/11/79
POSITION: MIDFIELDER
PREVIOUS CLUBS: FC HAKA, AUXERRE

A childhood Spurs fan, Teemu Tainio was delighted when he signed on at White Hart Lane in July 2005. Tottenham fans were soon to be just as happy that he'd joined. The attacking midfielder signed for Spurs from Auxerre where he had carved out a reputation as a driving force in the midfield of Guy Roux's stylish team. Comfortable with both feet and an accomplished international performer, Teemu is a fine passer of the ball and is a determined presence in any position across the midfield.

TOM HUDDLESTONE

DOB: 28/12/86
POSITION: DEFENDER/MIDFIELDER
PREVIOUS CLUBS: DERBY COUNTY,
WOLVES (LOAN)

There are few players who better typify Tottenham's policy in investing in the best young British talent than Tom Huddlestone. The defender-cum-midfielder was one of the most sought after players in the country when he signed on at White Hart Lane in July 2005. Expected to become a regular in the Spurs first team, Huddlestone has been honing his skills on loan at Wolverhampton Wanderers. At home both in the centre of defence and as holding midfielder, Tom plays a calm, measured game and displays a wide passing range as well as being powerful in the tackle.

YOUNG-PYO LEE

DOB: 23/4/77
POSITION: DEFENDER
PREVIOUS CLUBS: ANYANG LG CHEETAHS, PSV EINDHOVEN

When Young-Pyo Lee signed in August 2005 he was heralded by Martin Jol as the best left-back playing in Holland. The attack minded and tricky defender played in the South Korea side that reached the semi-finals of the World Cup in 2002 and has built on his reputation ever since. Making 32 appearances for Tottenham in the 2005/06 season, he was a leading member of his national side in the 2006 World Cup finals.

PLAYER OF THE YEAR
ROBBIE KEANE

When Robbie Keane stepped up to accept his award for Player of Season at the end of last term, he couldn't make himself heard over the fans singing his name.

And with good reason.

When Tottenham needed a goal in the second half of the season, more often than not it was the new Republic of Ireland captain who stepped up to bag the points.

At only 26, the Dubliner is a well travelled footballer, having played for Wolves, Coventry, Inter Milan and Leeds before signing on at White Hart Lane in 2003.

Fearsomely skilful and a scorer of sometimes spectacular goals, Robbie is a player who brings fans to their feet and fits in perfectly with the stylish traditions of Tottenham.

With the ball at his feet, Robbie is a match for anyone in the Premiership and his value to any team was underlined when Inter Milan president Massimo Moratti admitted he still regrets allowing him to leave the Serie A club.

So it was with both relief and delight that Spurs fans greeted the news that Keane had signed a four year extension to his contract.

Our player of the year said: "This is a club that is going places. I believe that and it is the reason why I signed here from Leeds in the first place.

"I had the feeling it was a club going in the right direction and I still believe this, especially with how the team are doing and the quality of the players that have been bought in."

And he paid tribute to the support he gets from the Spurs crowd, adding: "I've been lucky enough since I signed in that the fans have been tremendous to me. This is also my way of thanking them for their support. I am looking forward to the next four years now with Tottenham and the gaffer."

The gaffer certainly joins the fans in appreciating just what Robbie brings to the Spurs team.

Martin Jol said of his striker: "Robbie is important to us, a real team player and my second captain. He is a leader and has developed that quality."

A leader on the pitch who scores great goals and provides his team mates with chances.

No wonder Robbie Keane was Tottenham's player of the year.

AARON LENNON
YOUNG PLAYER OF THE YEAR

Few young players can have made such an impact in their first season with a new team than Aaron Lennon when he arrived at White Hart Lane.

Scoring vital goals, having opposing defenders for breakfast and winning a call up to the England World Cup Squad, Aaron Lennon is one of the most exciting young talents in the country. And he's well on his way to becoming a Tottenham legend.

With enough pace to worry even the quickest opponent, Lennon was already a hot prospect when he signed from Leeds but when he stepped in for the injured Wayne Routledge he very quickly made his presence felt.

Teammate Paul Robinson is certainly delighted to see the player he knew at Leeds living up to his potential at the Lane.

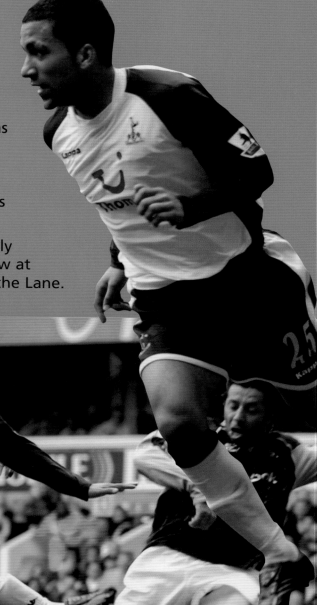

England's number one said: "One of the personal highlights for me this season is the development of Aaron Lennon – he's come on leaps and bounds.

"I was with Aaron for a long time at Leeds and to see what he's done this season has been fantastic."

That development was recognised by Spurs fans and by the PFA, who nominated him as one of the young players of the year.

And he impressed England coach Sven Goran Eriksson, who saw him as the kind of player who could set the world stage alight in Germany.

Before the cup, the national coach paid tribute to the valuable contribution the teenager can make to any team, saying: "Lennon has pace, beats people and is a good crosser. He is a very interesting player."

But his club manager, Martin Jol, is even happier to sing the praises of his exciting young winger.

"I think he can become more influential and we tell him that because at the age of 19 you can improve in every game," comments the Dutchman.

Adding: "To play for a club like Tottenham at White Hart Lane at that age, you want to improve and he wants to do that. We need that with all the young players, if they don't want to improve and develop, we will be a normal club – and we want to an exciting club."

And after a white hot season, Lennon capped it all by signing a new deal to keep him at the club until 2010.

On signing the contract, the young maestro said: "I'm thoroughly enjoying my football at Spurs and it's a great squad that I really feel part of."

And the fans are thoroughly enjoying watching him play in the great tradition of Tottenham Hotspur.

SPURS AT THE WORLD CUP

The World Cup ended in disappointment for Tottenham's England stars, but our internationalists enhanced their own reputations no end.

Speedy winger Aaron Lennon was one of the revelations of the tournament, coming on against Trinidad and Tobago to turn what could have been an embarrassing goalless draw into a 2-0 win.

The teenagers' pace and trickery became a vital weapon for England boss Sven Goran Eriksson and his arrival in the closing stages of matches was the cue for full-backs to start getting nervous.

Meanwhile, Spurs and England's number one, Paul Robinson, was the heart of one stingiest defences in the competition.

The Park Lane hero pulled off one of the saves of the tournament against Sweden and was often overlooked when it was time for praise to be lavished.

And while Jermaine Jenas didn't make an appearance his regular place in the squad marks him out as one of England's finest young midfield men.

One player that was to make a big impact on Spurs fans everywhere was Didier Zokora, who controlled the midfield for the Ivory Coast.

While the player known as the Maestro was unable to lead his side into the next round, his driving play and all round game put him at the top of many a Tottenham fans wanted list.

And by the end of the tournament, he had signed on to join the Jol revolution at White Hart Lane.

Left-back Lee Young Pyo may also have seen his side go out at the first hurdle, but the South Korean was one of the most impressive performers in the team that beat Togo and shocked finalists France.

YOUNG ENGLISH PLAYERS QUIZ

1 From which Championship club did we sign defender Tom Huddlestone?

2 Who also joined Spurs as part of the deal that brought Michael Dawson to the club?

3 Aaron Lennon netted against Bolton and which other team in the Premiership last season?

4 And against which country did Aaron make his international debut during the World Cup?

5 Paul Robinson, Aaron Lennon and which other Spurs player were in the England squad for the World Cup?

6 How much did the club pay West Ham for Michael Carrick?

7 Where did Wayne Routledge go on loan last season?

DID YOU KNOW

Spurs can count Fast Show star Paul Whitehouse, author Salman Rushdie, Goodfella's star Ray Liotta and comedian Paul Merton among their fans.

Gordon Durie scored Totteham's first goal in the newly formed Premiership in the 1992/93 season. Durie scored in a 2-2 draw with Crystal Palace.

Notts County were the first team to face Spurs at White Hart Lane. They were beaten 4-1 in a friendly on Monday, September 4, 1899.

Terry Fenwick scored against Tottenham in the 1982 FA Cup Final for Queens Park Rangers – he was later to join Spurs.

Spurs paid £99,999 for striker Jimmy Greaves so he wouldn't become the country's first six figure player.

Frank Bretell was Tottenham's first manager, leading the club for just one season in 1898/99.

MANSION DEAL

A new shirt and a new sponsor gave Tottenham the chance to kick off the new season and the push for European glory in style.

The Puma designed kit is a return to the classic Spurs style and will now bear the name of internet casino group Mansion.

As Spurs push on towards league and cup success, so they become a more attractive name for sponsors and Mansion were delighted to secure a four year, £34 million deal to be associated with the Lilywhites.

And Tottenham chairman Daniel Levy welcomed the deal, saying: "Tottenham has made progress both on and off the pitch in recent years which has put the club in a good position to improve its commercial partnerships and the new agreement marks a significant uplift."

SUMMER SIGNINGS

BENOIT ASSOU-EKOTTO

One of the most exciting talents in the French game, Benoit Assou-Ekotto signed for Tottenham from Lens.

The signing of the 22 year-old left back is a shining example of the Spurs policy of investing in the best young players world football has to offer.

Comfortable as both a left back and on the left side of midfield, Assou-Ekotto was being targeted by several Premiership clubs but was keen to join the Martin Jol revolution at White Hart Lane.

Spurs Sporting Director Damien Comolli was instrumental in the player's arrival and he commented: "He's regarded as one of the best prospects in French football and is an excellent signing for the club.

"The player is ambitious and has always wanted to play in English football. He was consistent in his commitment to us in the negotiations we had with Lens despite a lot of interest from other clubs and Lens being reluctant to let him go."

Benoit played regularly for Lens in Ligue 1 and is expected to provide manager Martin Jol with greater flexibility on the left flank.

DIMITAR BERBATOV

Under Martin Jol, Spurs have become renowned for snapping up the best young English and continental talent.

But when the chance comes to invest in a genuine world star, they're not shy in committing the resources.

Dimitar Berbatov arrived from Bayer Leverkusen with a big reputation and an impressive transfer fee, the deal believed to be costing £10.7 million.

A regular goal scorer for the Bundesliga club, Berbatov is also a prolific hitman on the international stage and was voted Bulgarian player of the year in 2002, 2004 and 2005.

Sporting director Damien Comolli was delighted with the audacious capture of one of the most sought after players in Europe.

"He is a tall, skilful, highly-talented striker who not only has a proven track record of being able to finish, but also of creating scoring opportunities for team mates," said Comolli.

And Berbatov was just as glad to join Spurs, turning down an offer from Manchester United to sign on at White Hart Lane.

He told the Spurs website: "Tottenham is a club that is building something special. The squad has some terrific young players, an excellent manager and coaching staff and I am looking forward to playing my part."

DIDIER ZOKORA

Every Spurs fan watching the World Cup will have noticed the commanding play of midfield general Didier Zokora and hoped the 25 year-old could be persuaded to sign for the Lillywhites. Thanks to the persistence of Sporting Director Damien Comolli, we were able to lure the former St Etienne man to White Hart Lane.

Principally a holding midfielder, Didier also has the drive to push forward in support of attacks and, as he showed for the Ivory Coast, has a cannon of a shot as well as an eye for a counter-attack-foiling challenge.

Manager Martin Jol was delighted to secure the player and commented: "Didier was regarded by a lot of people as one of the best midfield players going into the World Cup and he proved that in the group stage.

"A lot of clubs were after him, we had to compete for this services and he is a very good signing."

The stage is now set for Didier to step up and make the centre of the Tottenham midfield his domain.

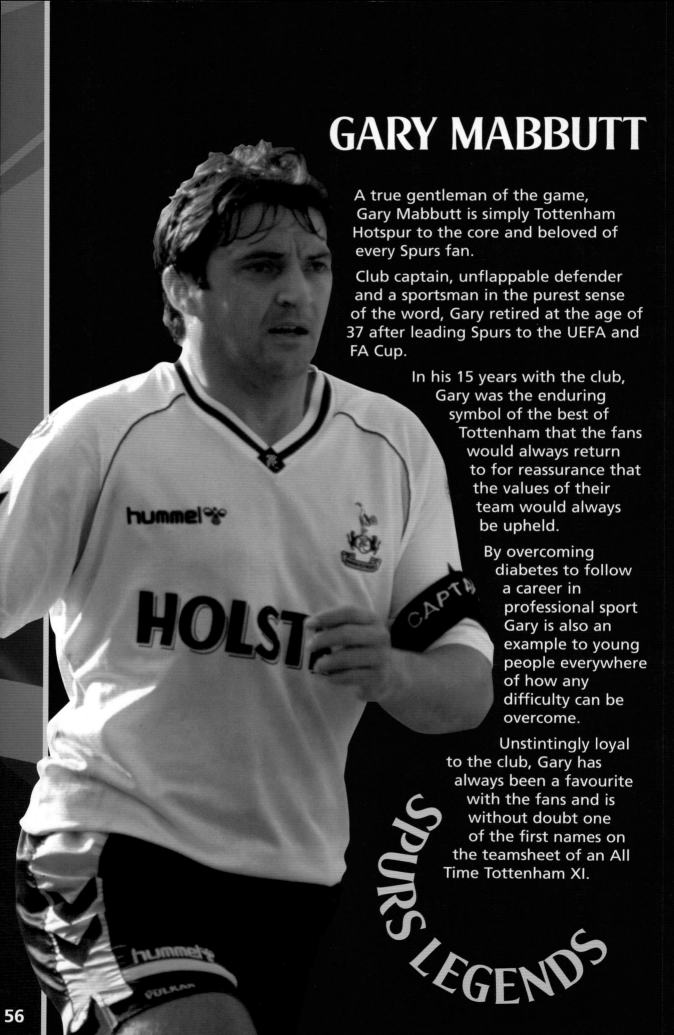

GARY MABBUTT

A true gentleman of the game, Gary Mabbutt is simply Tottenham Hotspur to the core and beloved of every Spurs fan.

Club captain, unflappable defender and a sportsman in the purest sense of the word, Gary retired at the age of 37 after leading Spurs to the UEFA and FA Cup.

In his 15 years with the club, Gary was the enduring symbol of the best of Tottenham that the fans would always return to for reassurance that the values of their team would always be upheld.

By overcoming diabetes to follow a career in professional sport Gary is also an example to young people everywhere of how any difficulty can be overcome.

Unstintingly loyal to the club, Gary has always been a favourite with the fans and is without doubt one of the first names on the teamsheet of an All Time Tottenham XI.

SPURS LEGENDS

GLENN HODDLE

The most gifted English player of his generation, Glenn Hoddle was a master with the ball at his feet. Indeed it sometimes appeared as though the ball was trying to please him. If that was by finding a team mate after cruising fifty yards through the air, then it would do it. Or if it was crashing into the net from an exquisite volley, then that was fine.

Glenn Hoddle was the Tottenham tradition distilled into a player who made the game look so easy it was almost embarrassing.

He was the player the 1980s England team should have been built around, he was a player who made other professionals stand back and applaud.

And when he joined Monaco in 1987 he took them to another level.

He's managed Swindon, Chelsea, England, Southampton, Tottenham and Wolverhampton, but to every Spurs fan he will always be the master of the ball and a Tottenham legend.

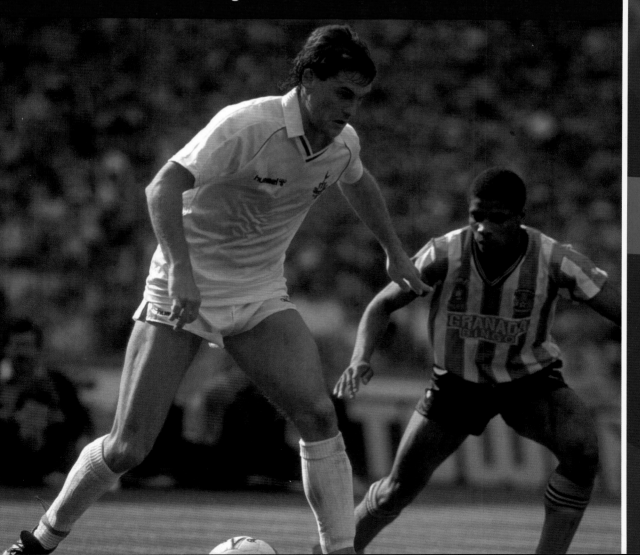

HISTORY OF SPURS

Stylish, push and run, entertaining, playing football the way it should be played – the tradition of Tottenham has endured since the great club was first formed.

The first club in the 20th century to win the league and FA Cup double, the first British club to win a European trophy, the home of Hoddle, Blanchflower, Mackay, Waddle, Lineker, Greaves, the history of Spurs is a long and glorious one.

Formed in 1882, Tottenham Hotspur moved to Northumberland Park in 1888 and turned professional in 1895, then in 1899 Spurs made their final move to the Tottenham High Road and White Hart Lane.

Settled in at the ground they still call home today, Spurs quickly made their mark on the English game, winning the 1901 FA Cup and becoming the only non-league side to do so.

With little competition for the young team in the Southern League, the White Hart Lane side were elected to the Second Division of the Football League in the 1908/09 season and immediately won promotion to the First Division.

But the following years weren't kind to Spurs, and when football was suspended with the coming of the First World War, they were languishing at the bottom of the table but ran out convincing Second Division champions in 1919/20 and bagged their second FA Cup in 1921.

It wasn't until after the Second World War that Spurs were to stamp their dominance back onto the English game, with the emergence of the famed 'push and run' side.

The brainchild of manager Arthur Rowe, the technique of laying the ball off and finding space to receive again was a novel one and was to form the basis of 'total football'.

With defences baffled by the high paced passing game, Spurs took the Second Division title in 49/50, before clinching the First Division in 50/51.

Spurs legend Bill Nicholson was one of the playing heroes of the side that took the title and his appointment as manager in October 1958 was to usher in the famous Glory Glory era.

Heralded as one of the finest English club sides of any era, the 1961 double winning side boasted players of the stature of Danny Blanchflower, Dave Mackay, Cliff Jones and Jimmy Greaves.

They would go on to win the FA Cup again in 1962 and the Cup Winner's Cup in 1963.

With age catching up on some of the side's stalwarts, Nicholson rebuilt the team, adding the 67 FA Cup, the League Cup in 71 and 73 and the UEFA Cup in 72 before he resigned in 1974.

The 80s brought the Keith Burkinshaw side that so memorably won the 1981 FA Cup, thanks to Ricky Villa's stunning solo goal - and retaining the cup the following season, thanks to the efforts of Steve Perryman, Glenn Hoddle, Ossie Ardiles and Steve Archibald.

That vintage side would also secure the 1984 UEFA Cup before Burkinshaw left to be replaced by Peter Shreeves.

In the 1986/87 season, under David Pleat, Spurs looked to again be mounting a league challenge, with the five man midfield of Hoddle, Ardiles, Hodge, Allen and Waddle supplying goal-scorer extraordinaire Clive Allen. But they faltered in the league and were cruelly denied in the FA Cup final by Coventry City.

The 1990s are often seen as a barren spell for the boys from White Hart Lane, the 1991 FA cup and the 1999 Worthington Cup the only silverware to show for a decade of endeavour.

But the fans had the chance to watch the incomparable skills of Paul Gascoigne, David Ginola, Jurgen Klinsmann, Gary Lineker and Teddy Sheringham as the club struggled to impose itself on the league.

With the dawning of a new century Tottenham have pushed on and are once again one of the leading clubs in the English game, narrowly missing Champions League qualification in their first full season under Martin Jol.

But the new dawn looks like being a bright one and the Glory Glory days can come back to N17.

HONOURS

FOOTBALL LEAGUE FIRST DIVISION CHAMPIONS:

1950/51, 1960/61

FOOTBALL LEAGUE SECOND DIVISION CHAMPIONS:

1919/20, 1949/50

FA CUP:

1900/01, 1920/21, 1960/61, 1961/62, 1966/67, 1980/81, 1981/82, 1990/91

LEAGUE CUP:

1970/71, 1972/73, 1998/99

FA CHARITY SHIELD:

1920/21, 1951/52, 1961/62, 1962/63, 1967/68, 1981/82, 1991/92

UEFA CUP:

1971/72, 1983/84

EUROPEAN CUP WINNERS' CUP:

1962/63

QUIZ ANSWERS

SEASON QUIZ (Page 19)

1) Ledley King, Robbie Keane
2) Jermaine Jenas, Paul Stalteri, Mark De Vries
3) Roma
4) Danny Murphy
5) Charlton Athletic
6) Aaron Lennon
7) Wigan Athletic

SPOT THE DIFFERENCE (Page 22)

1) Blue sweatband,
   Red logo on glasses,
   Logos from socks missing

2) Dot missing from Thomson logo,
   Wrist band missing,
   Logo from ball missing

WORDSEARCH (Page 23)

YOUNG ENGLISH PLAYERS QUIZ (Page 48)

1) Derby County
2) Andy Reid
3) Birmingham City
4) Trinidad and Tobago
5) Jermain Jenas
6) £2.75 million
7) Portsmouth

CROSSWORD (Page 26)

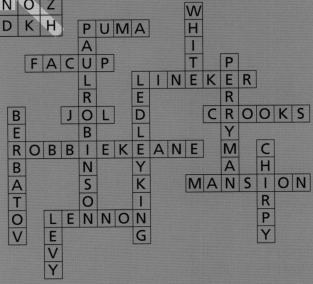